Contents

Part One

Keep a record of all the books you read.

Part Two

Book review pages to go into more detail.

Part Three

Build your TBR list so that you've always got your next read.

Reading Log

So many books, so little time.....

Book Title	Author	Rating	Date Started	Date Finished
		☆ ☆ ☆ ☆ ☆		
		☆ ☆ ☆ ☆ ☆		
		☆ ☆ ☆ ☆ ☆		
		☆ ☆ ☆ ☆ ☆		
		☆ ☆ ☆ ☆ ☆		
		☆ ☆ ☆ ☆ ☆		
		☆ ☆ ☆ ☆ ☆		
		☆ ☆ ☆ ☆ ☆		
		☆ ☆ ☆ ☆ ☆		
		☆ ☆ ☆ ☆ ☆		
		☆ ☆ ☆ ☆ ☆		
		☆ ☆ ☆ ☆ ☆		
		☆ ☆ ☆ ☆ ☆		
		☆ ☆ ☆ ☆ ☆		
		☆ ☆ ☆ ☆ ☆		
		☆ ☆ ☆ ☆ ☆		
		☆ ☆ ☆ ☆ ☆		
		☆ ☆ ☆ ☆ ☆		
		☆ ☆ ☆ ☆ ☆		
		☆ ☆ ☆ ☆ ☆		
		☆ ☆ ☆ ☆ ☆		
		☆ ☆ ☆ ☆ ☆		
		☆ ☆ ☆ ☆ ☆		
		☆ ☆ ☆ ☆ ☆		
		☆ ☆ ☆ ☆ ☆		
		☆ ☆ ☆ ☆ ☆		
		☆ ☆ ☆ ☆ ☆		
		☆ ☆ ☆ ☆ ☆		

Reading Log

So many books, so little time.....

Book Title	Author	Rating	Date Started	Date Finished
		☆ ☆ ☆ ☆ ☆		
		☆ ☆ ☆ ☆ ☆		
		☆ ☆ ☆ ☆ ☆		
		☆ ☆ ☆ ☆ ☆		
		☆ ☆ ☆ ☆ ☆		
		☆ ☆ ☆ ☆ ☆		
		☆ ☆ ☆ ☆ ☆		
		☆ ☆ ☆ ☆ ☆		
		☆ ☆ ☆ ☆ ☆		
		☆ ☆ ☆ ☆ ☆		
		☆ ☆ ☆ ☆ ☆		
		☆ ☆ ☆ ☆ ☆		
		☆ ☆ ☆ ☆ ☆		
		☆ ☆ ☆ ☆ ☆		
		☆ ☆ ☆ ☆ ☆		
		☆ ☆ ☆ ☆ ☆		
		☆ ☆ ☆ ☆ ☆		
		☆ ☆ ☆ ☆ ☆		
		☆ ☆ ☆ ☆ ☆		
		☆ ☆ ☆ ☆ ☆		
		☆ ☆ ☆ ☆ ☆		
		☆ ☆ ☆ ☆ ☆		
		☆ ☆ ☆ ☆ ☆		
		☆ ☆ ☆ ☆ ☆		
		☆ ☆ ☆ ☆ ☆		
		☆ ☆ ☆ ☆ ☆		
		☆ ☆ ☆ ☆ ☆		
		☆ ☆ ☆ ☆ ☆		
		☆ ☆ ☆ ☆ ☆		

Reading Log

So many books, so little time.....

Book Title	Author	Rating	Date Started	Date Finished
		☆ ☆ ☆ ☆ ☆		
		☆ ☆ ☆ ☆ ☆		
		☆ ☆ ☆ ☆ ☆		
		☆ ☆ ☆ ☆ ☆		
		☆ ☆ ☆ ☆ ☆		
		☆ ☆ ☆ ☆ ☆		
		☆ ☆ ☆ ☆ ☆		
		☆ ☆ ☆ ☆ ☆		
		☆ ☆ ☆ ☆ ☆		
		☆ ☆ ☆ ☆ ☆		
		☆ ☆ ☆ ☆ ☆		
		☆ ☆ ☆ ☆ ☆		
		☆ ☆ ☆ ☆ ☆		
		☆ ☆ ☆ ☆ ☆		
		☆ ☆ ☆ ☆ ☆		
		☆ ☆ ☆ ☆ ☆		
		☆ ☆ ☆ ☆ ☆		
		☆ ☆ ☆ ☆ ☆		
		☆ ☆ ☆ ☆ ☆		
		☆ ☆ ☆ ☆ ☆		
		☆ ☆ ☆ ☆ ☆		
		☆ ☆ ☆ ☆ ☆		
		☆ ☆ ☆ ☆ ☆		
		☆ ☆ ☆ ☆ ☆		
		☆ ☆ ☆ ☆ ☆		
		☆ ☆ ☆ ☆ ☆		
		☆ ☆ ☆ ☆ ☆		
		☆ ☆ ☆ ☆ ☆		

Reading Log

So many books, so little time.....

Book Title	Author	Rating	Date Started	Date Finished
		☆ ☆ ☆ ☆ ☆		
		☆ ☆ ☆ ☆ ☆		
		☆ ☆ ☆ ☆ ☆		
		☆ ☆ ☆ ☆ ☆		
		☆ ☆ ☆ ☆ ☆		
		☆ ☆ ☆ ☆ ☆		
		☆ ☆ ☆ ☆ ☆		
		☆ ☆ ☆ ☆ ☆		
		☆ ☆ ☆ ☆ ☆		
		☆ ☆ ☆ ☆ ☆		
		☆ ☆ ☆ ☆ ☆		
		☆ ☆ ☆ ☆ ☆		
		☆ ☆ ☆ ☆ ☆		
		☆ ☆ ☆ ☆ ☆		
		☆ ☆ ☆ ☆ ☆		
		☆ ☆ ☆ ☆ ☆		
		☆ ☆ ☆ ☆ ☆		
		☆ ☆ ☆ ☆ ☆		
		☆ ☆ ☆ ☆ ☆		
		☆ ☆ ☆ ☆ ☆		
		☆ ☆ ☆ ☆ ☆		
		☆ ☆ ☆ ☆ ☆		
		☆ ☆ ☆ ☆ ☆		
		☆ ☆ ☆ ☆ ☆		
		☆ ☆ ☆ ☆ ☆		
		☆ ☆ ☆ ☆ ☆		
		☆ ☆ ☆ ☆ ☆		

Reading Log

So many books, so little time.....

Book Title	Author	Rating	Date Started	Date Finished
		☆ ☆ ☆ ☆ ☆		
		☆ ☆ ☆ ☆ ☆		
		☆ ☆ ☆ ☆ ☆		
		☆ ☆ ☆ ☆ ☆		
		☆ ☆ ☆ ☆ ☆		
		☆ ☆ ☆ ☆ ☆		
		☆ ☆ ☆ ☆ ☆		
		☆ ☆ ☆ ☆ ☆		
		☆ ☆ ☆ ☆ ☆		
		☆ ☆ ☆ ☆ ☆		
		☆ ☆ ☆ ☆ ☆		
		☆ ☆ ☆ ☆ ☆		
		☆ ☆ ☆ ☆ ☆		
		☆ ☆ ☆ ☆ ☆		
		☆ ☆ ☆ ☆ ☆		
		☆ ☆ ☆ ☆ ☆		
		☆ ☆ ☆ ☆ ☆		
		☆ ☆ ☆ ☆ ☆		
		☆ ☆ ☆ ☆ ☆		
		☆ ☆ ☆ ☆ ☆		
		☆ ☆ ☆ ☆ ☆		
		☆ ☆ ☆ ☆ ☆		
		☆ ☆ ☆ ☆ ☆		
		☆ ☆ ☆ ☆ ☆		
		☆ ☆ ☆ ☆ ☆		
		☆ ☆ ☆ ☆ ☆		
		☆ ☆ ☆ ☆ ☆		

Book Reviews

Book Review

Name of Book ....

Author: ....

Book Type: eg. ebook, audio
or paperback etc ....

Start Date: .... End Date:: ....

Genre: ....

Rating: ☆ ☆ ☆ ☆ ☆ DNF

General Storyline ....

....

....

....

....

What I liked about it

....

....

....

....

....

....

....

What I disliked about it

....

....

....

....

....

....

....

Overall thoughts;

_____

_____

_____

_____

_____

_____

_____

_____

If you don't like to read, you havent found the right book - JK Rowling

Favourite Quotes/Lines;

_____

_____

_____

_____

_____

_____

_____

_____

_____

If a book is well written, I always find it too short - Jane Austen

Other things I want
to say about this book

Today a reader, tomorrow a leader - Margaret Fuller

The world belongs to those who read - Rick Holland

Book Review

Name of Book ....

Author: ....

Book Type: eg. ebook, audio
or paperback etc ....

Start Date: .... End Date:: ....

Genre: ....

Rating: ☆ ☆ ☆ ☆ ☆ DNF

General Storyline ....
....
....
....
....

What I liked about it

What I disliked about it

Overall thoughts;

_____

_____

_____

_____

_____

_____

_____

_____

_____

If you don't like to read, you havent found the right book - JK Rowling

Favourite Quotes/Lines;

_____

_____

_____

_____

_____

_____

_____

_____

_____

If a book is well written, I always find it too short - Jane Austen

Other things I want
to say about this book

Today a reader,
tomorrow a leader -
Margaret Fuller

The world belongs to those
who read - Rick Holland

Book Review

Name of Book ....

Author: ....

Book Type: eg. ebook, audio or paperback etc ....

Start Date: .... End Date:: ....

Genre: ....

Rating: ☆ ☆ ☆ ☆ ☆ DNF

General Storyline ....

....

....

....

....

What I liked about it

....
....
....
....
....
....
....

What I disliked about it

....
....
....
....
....
....
....

Overall thoughts;

If you don't like to read,
you haven't found the
right book – JK Rowling

Favourite Quotes/Lines;

If a book is
well written,
I always find
it too short –
Jane Austen

Other things I want
to say about this book

Today a reader, tomorrow a leader - Margaret Fuller

The world belongs to those who read - Rick Holland

Book Review

Name of Book ....

Author: ....

Book Type: eg. ebook, audio or paperback etc ....

Start Date: .... End Date:: ....

Genre: ....

Rating: ☆ ☆ ☆ ☆ ☆   DNF

General Storyline ....

....

....

....

....

What I liked about it

What I disliked about it

Overall thoughts;

....
....
....
....
....
....
....
....
....
....

If you don't like to read, you haven't found the right book - JK Rowling

Favourite Quotes/Lines;

....
....
....
....
....
....
....
....
....
....

If a book is well written, I always find it too short - Jane Austen

Other things I want
to say about this book

Today a reader, tomorrow a leader – Margaret Fuller

The world belongs to those who read – Rick Holland

Book Review

Name of Book ....

Author: ....

Book Type: eg. ebook, audio or paperback etc ....

Start Date: .... End Date:: ....

Genre: ....

Rating: ☆ ☆ ☆ ☆ ☆ DNF

General Storyline ....

....

....

....

....

....

What I liked about it

....

....

....

....

....

....

....

What I disliked about it

....

....

....

....

....

....

....

Overall thoughts;

....

....

....

....

....

....

....

....

....

If you don't like to read, you haven't found the right book - JK Rowling

Favourite Quotes/Lines;

....

....

....

....

....

....

....

....

If a book is well written, I always find it too short - Jane Austen

Other things I want
to say about this book

Today a reader,
tomorrow a leader -
Margaret Fuller

The world belongs to those
who read - Rick Holland

Book Review

Name of Book ....

Author: ....

Book Type: eg. ebook, audio or paperback etc ....

Start Date: .... End Date:: ....

Genre: ....

Rating: ☆ ☆ ☆ ☆ ☆ DNF

General Storyline ....
....
....
....
....

What I liked about it

What I disliked about it

Overall thoughts;

....
....
....
....
....
....
....
....
....
....

If you don't like to read, you haven't found the right book - JK Rowling

Favourite Quotes/Lines;

....
....
....
....
....
....
....
....
....

If a book is well written, I always find it too short - Jane Austen

Other things I want
to say about this book

Today a reader,
tomorrow a leader -
Margaret Fuller

The world belongs to those
who read - Rick Holland

Book Review

Name of Book
....

Author:
....

Book Type: eg. ebook, audio
or paperback etc
....

Start Date: .... End Date:: ....

Genre:
....

Rating: ☆ ☆ ☆ ☆ ☆   DNF

General Storyline ....

....

....

....

....

What I liked about it

What I disliked about it

Overall thoughts;

....

....

....

....

....

....

....

....

....

....

If you don't like to read, you havent found the right book -JK Rowling

Favourite Quotes/Lines;

....

....

....

....

....

....

....

....

....

....

....

If a book is well written, I always find it too short - Jane Austen

Other things I want
to say about this book

Today a reader, tomorrow a leader – Margaret Fuller

The world belongs to those who read – Rick Holland

Book Review

Name of Book ....

Author: ....

Book Type: eg. ebook, audio or paperback etc ....

Start Date: .... End Date:: ....

Genre: ....

Rating: ☆ ☆ ☆ ☆ ☆ DNF

General Storyline ....

....

....

....

....

What I liked about it

....

....

....

....

....

....

What I disliked about it

....

....

....

....

....

....

Overall thoughts;

....

....

....

....

....

....

....

....

....

If you don't like to read, you havent found the right book - JK Rowling

Favourite Quotes/Lines;

....

....

....

....

....

....

....

....

If a book is well written, I always find it too short - Jane Austen

Other things I want
to say about this book

Today a reader,
tomorrow a leader –
Margaret Fuller

The world belongs to those
who read – Rick Holland

Book Review

Name of Book
....

Author:
....

Book Type: eg. ebook, audio
             or paperback etc
....

Start Date: ....   End Date:: ....

Genre:
....

Rating: ☆ ☆ ☆ ☆ ☆   DNF

General Storyline ....

....

....

....

....

What I liked about it

....
....
....
....
....
....
....
....

What I disliked about it

....
....
....
....
....
....
....
....

Overall thoughts;

If you don't like to read, you haven't found the right book - JK Rowling

Favourite Quotes/Lines;

If a book is well written, I always find it too short - Jane Austen

Other things I want
to say about this book

Today a reader, tomorrow a leader - Margaret Fuller

The world belongs to those who read - Rick Holland

Book Review

Name of Book

....

Author:

....

Book Type: eg. ebook, audio or paperback etc

....

Start Date: .... End Date:: ....

Genre:

....

Rating: ☆ ☆ ☆ ☆ ☆ DNF

General Storyline ....

....

....

....

....

What I liked about it

....

....

....

....

....

....

....

What I disliked about it

....

....

....

....

....

....

....

Overall thoughts;

If you don't like to read, you haven't found the right book - JK Rowling

Favourite Quotes/Lines;

If a book is well written, I always find it too short - Jane Austen

Other things I want
to say about this book

Today a reader,
tomorrow a leader -
Margaret Fuller

The world belongs to those
who read - Rick Holland

Book Review

Name of Book ....

Author: ....

Book Type: eg. ebook, audio or paperback etc ....

Start Date: .... End Date:: ....

Genre: ....

Rating: ☆ ☆ ☆ ☆ ☆   DNF

General Storyline ....

....

....

....

....

What I liked about it

....

....

....

....

....

....

....

What I disliked about it

....

....

....

....

....

....

....

Overall thoughts;

If you don't like to read, you haven't found the right book - JK Rowling

Favourite Quotes/Lines;

If a book is well written, I always find it too short - Jane Austen

Other things I want
to say about this book

Today a reader, tomorrow a leader - Margaret Fuller

The world belongs to those who read - Rick Holland

Book Review

Name of Book
....

Author:
....

Book Type: eg. ebook, audio or paperback etc
....

Start Date: .... End Date:: ....

Genre:
....

Rating: ☆ ☆ ☆ ☆ ☆   DNF

General Storyline ....
....
....
....
....

What I liked about it

....
....
....
....
....
....
....

What I disliked about it

....
....
....
....
....
....
....

Overall thoughts;

....

....

....

....

....

....

....

....

....

*If you don't like to read,
you haven't found the
right book - JK Rowling*

Favourite Quotes/Lines;

....

....

....

....

....

....

....

....

*If a book is
well written,
I always find
it too short -
Jane Austen*

Other things I want
to say about this book

Today a reader,
tomorrow a leader -
Margaret Fuller

The world belongs to those
who read - Rick Holland

Book Review

Name of Book ....

Author: ....

Book Type: eg. ebook, audio or paperback etc ....

Start Date: .... End Date:: ....

Genre: ....

Rating: ☆ ☆ ☆ ☆ ☆ DNF

General Storyline ....

....

....

....

....

What I liked about it

....

....

....

....

....

....

....

What I disliked about it

....

....

....

....

....

....

....

Overall thoughts;

....
....
....
....
....
....
....
....
....
....
....

If you don't like to read, you havent found the right book - JK Rowling

Favourite Quotes/Lines;

....
....
....
....
....
....
....
....
....
....
....

If a book is well written, I always find it too short - Jane Austen

Other things I want
to say about this book

Today a reader, tomorrow a leader - Margaret Fuller

The world belongs to those who read - Rick Holland

Book Review

Name of Book ....

Author: ....

Book Type: eg. ebook, audio or paperback etc ....

Start Date: .... End Date:: ....

Genre: ....

Rating: ☆ ☆ ☆ ☆ ☆ DNF

General Storyline ....

....

....

....

....

What I liked about it

....

....

....

....

....

....

....

What I disliked about it

....

....

....

....

....

....

....

Overall thoughts;

If you don't like to read, you haven't found the right book - JK Rowling

Favourite Quotes/Lines;

If a book is well written, I always find it too short - Jane Austen

Other things I want
to say about this book

Today a reader,
tomorrow a leader -
Margaret Fuller

The world belongs to those
who read - Rick Holland

Book Review

Name of Book ....

Author: ....

Book Type: *eg. ebook, audio or paperback etc* ....

Start Date: .... End Date:: ....

Genre: ....

Rating: ☆ ☆ ☆ ☆ ☆ DNF

General Storyline ....

....

....

....

....

What I liked about it

....

....

....

....

....

....

....

What I disliked about it

....

....

....

....

....

....

....

Overall thoughts;

....

....

....

....

....

....

....

....

....

If you don't like to read, you haven't found the right book - JK Rowling

Favourite Quotes/Lines;

....

....

....

....

....

....

....

....

If a book is well written, I always find it too short - Jane Austen

Other things I want
to say about this book

Today a reader,
tomorrow a leader -
Margaret Fuller

The world belongs to those
who read - Rick Holland

Book Review

Name of Book ....

Author: ....

Book Type: eg. ebook, audio or paperback etc ....

Start Date: .... End Date:: ....

Genre: ....

Rating: ☆ ☆ ☆ ☆ ☆ DNF

General Storyline ....

....

....

....

....

What I liked about it

....

....

....

....

....

....

....

What I disliked about it

....

....

....

....

....

....

....

Overall thoughts;

....

....

....

....

....

....

....

....

....

If you don't like to read, you haven't found the right book - JK Rowling

Favourite Quotes/Lines;

....

....

....

....

....

....

....

....

....

If a book is well written, I always find it too short - Jane Austen

Other things I want
to say about this book

Today a reader,
tomorrow a leader -
Margaret Fuller

The world belongs to those
who read - Rick Holland

Book Review

Name of Book
....

Author:
....

Book Type: eg. ebook, audio
or paperback etc
....

Start Date: .... End Date:: ....

Genre:
....

Rating: ☆ ☆ ☆ ☆ ☆ DNF

General Storyline ....

....

....

....

....

What I liked about it

😊

....

....

....

....

....

....

....

....

What I disliked about it

☹

....

....

....

....

....

....

....

Overall thoughts;

If you don't like to read, you havent found the right book - JK Rowling

Favourite Quotes/Lines;

If a book is well written, I always find it too short - Jane Austen

Other things I want
to say about this book

Today a reader, tomorrow a leader - Margaret Fuller

The world belongs to those who read - Rick Holland

Book Review

Name of Book ....

Author: ....

Book Type: eg. ebook, audio or paperback etc ....

Start Date: .... **End Date::** ....

Genre: ....

Rating: ☆ ☆ ☆ ☆ ☆   DNF

General Storyline ....

....

....

....

....

What I liked about it

....

....

....

....

....

....

....

What I disliked about it

....

....

....

....

....

....

....

Overall thoughts;

....

....

....

....

....

....

....

....

....

*If you don't like to read,
you havent found the
right book - JK Rowling*

Favourite Quotes/Lines;

....

....

....

....

....

....

....

....

*If a book is
well written,
I always find
it too short -
Jane Austen*

Other things I want
to say about this book

Today a reader, tomorrow a leader - Margaret Fuller

The world belongs to those who read - Rick Holland

Book Review

Name of Book ....

Author: ....

Book Type: eg. ebook, audio or paperback etc ....

Start Date: .... End Date:: ....

Genre: ....

Rating: ☆ ☆ ☆ ☆ ☆   DNF

General Storyline ....

....

....

....

....

What I liked about it	What I disliked about it

Overall thoughts;

....

....

....

....

....

....

....

....

....

If you don't like to read, you haven't found the right book - JK Rowling

Favourite Quotes/Lines;

....

....

....

....

....

....

....

....

....

If a book is well written, I always find it too short - Jane Austen

Other things I want
to say about this book

Today a reader, tomorrow a leader - Margaret Fuller

The world belongs to those who read - Rick Holland

Book Review

Name of Book

Author:

Book Type: eg. ebook, audio or paperback etc

Start Date: End Date::

Genre:

Rating: ☆ ☆ ☆ ☆ ☆   DNF

General Storyline

What I liked about it

What I disliked about it

Overall thoughts;

If you don't like to read, you haven't found the right book - JK Rowling

Favourite Quotes/Lines;

If a book is well written, I always find it too short - Jane Austen

Other things I want
to say about this book

Today a reader, tomorrow a leader – Margaret Fuller

The world belongs to those who read – Rick Holland

Book Review

Name of Book ....

Author: ....

Book Type: eg. ebook, audio or paperback etc ....

Start Date: .... End Date:: ....

Genre: ....

Rating: ☆ ☆ ☆ ☆ ☆ DNF

General Storyline ....

....

....

....

....

What I liked about it

....

....

....

....

....

....

....

What I disliked about it

....

....

....

....

....

....

....

Overall thoughts;

If you don't like to read, you haven't found the right book - JK Rowling

Favourite Quotes/Lines;

If a book is well written, I always find it too short - Jane Austen

Other things I want
to say about this book

Today a reader, tomorrow a leader - Margaret Fuller

The world belongs to those who read - Rick Holland

Book Review

Name of Book

Author:

Book Type: eg. ebook, audio or paperback etc

Start Date: End Date::

Genre:

Rating: ☆ ☆ ☆ ☆ ☆   DNF

General Storyline

What I liked about it

What I disliked about it

Overall thoughts;

....

....

....

....

....

....

....

....

....

If you don't like to read, you havent found the right book - JK Rowling

Favourite Quotes/Lines;

....

....

....

....

....

....

....

....

....

If a book is well written, I always find it too short - Jane Austen

Other things I want
to say about this book

*Today a reader,
tomorrow a leader –
Margaret Fuller*

*The world belongs to those
who read – Rick Holland*

Book Review

Name of Book ....

Author: ....

Book Type: *eg. ebook, audio or paperback etc* ....

Start Date: .... End Date:: ....

Genre: ....

Rating: ☆ ☆ ☆ ☆ ☆ DNF

General Storyline ....

....

....

....

....

What I liked about it

....

....

....

....

....

....

....

What I disliked about it

....

....

....

....

....

....

Overall thoughts;

....

....

....

....

....

....

....

....

If you don't like to read, you havent found the right book - JK Rowling

Favourite Quotes/Lines;

....

....

....

....

....

....

....

....

If a book is well written, I always find it too short - Jane Austen

Other things I want
to say about this book

Today a reader,
tomorrow a leader -
Margaret Fuller

The world belongs to those
who read - Rick Holland

Book Review

Name of Book

Author:

Book Type: eg. ebook, audio or paperback etc

Start Date: End Date::

Genre:

Rating: ☆ ☆ ☆ ☆ ☆ DNF

General Storyline

What I liked about it

What I disliked about it

Overall thoughts;

....

....

....

....

....

....

....

....

....

If you don't like to read, you haven't found the right book - JK Rowling

Favourite Quotes/Lines;

....

....

....

....

....

....

....

....

....

If a book is well written, I always find it too short - Jane Austen

Other things I want
to say about this book

Today a reader, tomorrow a leader - Margaret Fuller

The world belongs to those who read - Rick Holland

Book Review

Name of Book ....

Author: ....

Book Type: eg. ebook, audio or paperback etc ....

Start Date: .... **End Date::** ....

Genre: ....

Rating: ☆ ☆ ☆ ☆ ☆ DNF

General Storyline ....

....

....

....

....

What I liked about it

....

....

....

....

....

....

....

What I disliked about it

....

....

....

....

....

....

....

Overall thoughts;

If you don't like to read, you havent found the right book -JK Rowling

Favourite Quotes/Lines;

If a book is well written, I always find it too short - Jane Austen

Other things I want
to say about this book

Today a reader, tomorrow a leader - Margaret Fuller

The world belongs to those who read - Rick Holland

TBR List

(To be read)

Book Title	Author	Who Recommended	Date Added	Where do I buy?	Cost

Books are a uniquely portable magic —
Stephen King

TBR List
(To be read)

Book Title	Author	Who Recommended	Date Added	Where do I buy?	Cost

Books are a uniquely portable magic –
Stephen King

TBR List

(To be read)

Book Title	Author	Who Recommended	Date Added	Where do I buy?	Cost

Books are a uniquely portable magic — Stephen King

TBR List

(To be read)

Book Title	Author	Who Recommended	Date Added	Where do I buy?	Cost

Books are a uniquely
portable magic -
Stephen King

TBR List

(To be read)

Book Title	Author	Who Recommended	Date Added	Where do I buy?	Cost

Books are a uniquely portable magic —
Stephen King

TBR List
(To be read)

Book Title	Author	Who Recommended	Date Added	Where do I buy?	Cost

Books are a uniquely portable magic –
Stephen King

Printed in Poland
by Amazon Fulfillment
Poland Sp. z o.o., Wrocław
07 December 2022